BOOKS BY PETER DALE

Verse

Under the Breath

Local Habitation

Diffractions: New and Collected Poems

Aquatints

Penumbral

Prose

Peter Dale in Conversation with Cynthia Haven

EARTHLY USE

EARTHLY USE
Poems 2018–2020

PETER DALE

For Roland and Anna

Editor: Owen Judd

Illustrator: Nick Davies

My blithy and beaces

Peter Dale

The Minilith Press
Cardiff

Published by

The Minilith Press, 2020

11 Heol Y Gors, Whitchurch, Cardiff, CF14 1HF

Tel.: 02920 520 244

© Peter Dale 2020. Illustrations © Nick Davies 2020.

Peter Dale has asserted his right under the Copyright, Design and Patents Act, 1988 to be identified as the author of this work.

ISBN: 978-0-9929875-6-5

British Library Catalogue in Publishing Data.

A catalogue record of the book is available from the British Library.

All rights reserved. Except for purposes of review no part of this book may be reproduced, stored in a retrieval system or transmitted in any means without the express permission of the publisher.

Acknowledgements

Versions of some of these poems first appeared in Acumen and Agenda.

The translation of Louis Aragon's 'Richard II Quarante' was first published by Hippopotamus Press, in Narrow Straits.

Printed and bound in Cardiff by Abbey Book Binding and Printing Ltd, Gabalfa, Cardiff, CF14 3AY.

FOR KIM AND GARETH

CONTENTS
indicates entry in the Notes

HOME FRONT	11
Second Childhood	11
Blackout*	12
Whereabouts*	13
Richard II, Forty*	14
HOME BASE	17
Flower-bound	17
Taken as Read*	18
Cryptograph	19
Mementos*	20
TALKING SHOP	21
A Lay of the Last Retainer*	21
Bar-Room Chat*	22
Some Dream Team*	23
Cutting Edge of Dream	24
Idle Talk	25
Dream On	26
Afterword	27
DRAGONIAN MEASURES	29
The First Welsh Dragon	29
Smoky	35
Dragon Flies?	39
ON THE MARGINS	40
Greetings	40
Inspiration	40
Virile Viruses	40
Dress-Sense	41
Prospects	41
Communication	41
Soliloquy	41
Geosophy	42
Winter Solstice	42
Translation Workshop	43
Envoi	44

ILLUSTRATIONS
The number in italics indicate the pages illustrated

Noughts and Crosses	*17*	16
The Green Dragon	*29*	28
Cranberry Bath	*29*	31
The Red Dragon	*35*	34
Dragon Flies?	*39*	38
Poinsettia	*18*	Front Cover
Roses	*18*	Back Cover

NOTES   45

ABOUT THE AUTHOR   47

HOME FRONT

SECOND CHILDHOOD

Cumulus cloud, like great tractor tyre tracks
through drifts of snow, climbing the blue sky.
I sit down in the window bay, relax,
and watch the clouds of childhood dawdle by.
A movement catches the corner of my eye:
leaves of the shrubs start bickering with the fence,
and their shadow leaves – birds that will not fly.
The cumulus, as they bicker, grows immense.

This cumulus doesn't kid me. It was the Blitz:
the daylight air-raids, ack-ack, barrage-balloons,
the Heinkels, Spitfires, searchlights, bombers' moons.
– My mates, post-war, built Spitfire balsa kits.
But once the props unwound their planes would stall.
– These clouds mime: fly away, Peter; flown away, Paul.

BLACKOUT*

The noughts-and-crosses grid of searchlight beams,
our beam-feast secret in the blacked-out room.
Dad was a warden checking on blackout gleams.
We felt the street was struck with every boom.
The milk-float wailed like starting siren screams.
We ran to shops to dodge the coming doom.
We walked the plank across the rain-made streams.
Teacher read to us in the shelter's gloom.

One breakfast, happy dad said it was peace.
I asked him how he knew: across the way
the neighbours took round pigswill, chicken-mash
as always. On the News, dad said. Today,
I said, without the War the News would cease,
too young to guess the Allies soon would clash.

WHEREABOUTS

Not Smith's farm where the barrage-balloon was downed.
(We kids were sent to help in its deflation.)
No rugby or football pitches, no cricket ground.
No trace of horticulture or cultivation.
A landscape where some big events took place:
say, village fête, or midsummer country 'fayre',
Neither where I'd have ever shown my face.
Midnight grassland, grass and more grass. But where?

Now this anonymous landscape from a dream
dislocates day with its vast field quite blank,
inveigling mind to see the ox-bow stream
with the neglected copse on the far bank
from where we saw the doodlebug and hid.
It drags me back to war-time as a kid.

RICHARD II FORTY * (after Louis Aragon)

My country now is like a barge
Left by the haulers to the reef
And I am like that king in charge
Of more misfortune than belief
Still am I king of all my grief

Now living's no more than a dodge
For tears the wind's no handkerchief
In all I love my hate must lodge
What I have lost gives them relief
Still am I king of all my grief

The heart knows how to beat no more
The blood just stirs so cold and brief
Let two and two not add to four
When Grundy says fly like a thief
Still am I king of all my grief

Whether the sun should live or die
The colours wither from the leaf
Sweet Paris of my youth, goodbye
And Quai-aux-Fleurs in spray and sheaf
Still am I king of all my grief

Desert the woods, the fountains flee
You birds so quarrelsome be brief
Your songs are sent to Coventry
The bird-catcher reigns as chief
Still am I king of all my grief

There is a time to suffer pain
When Joan brought Vaucouleurs relief
Oh, cut France into shreds again
The light was pallid on the leaf
Still am I king of all my grief

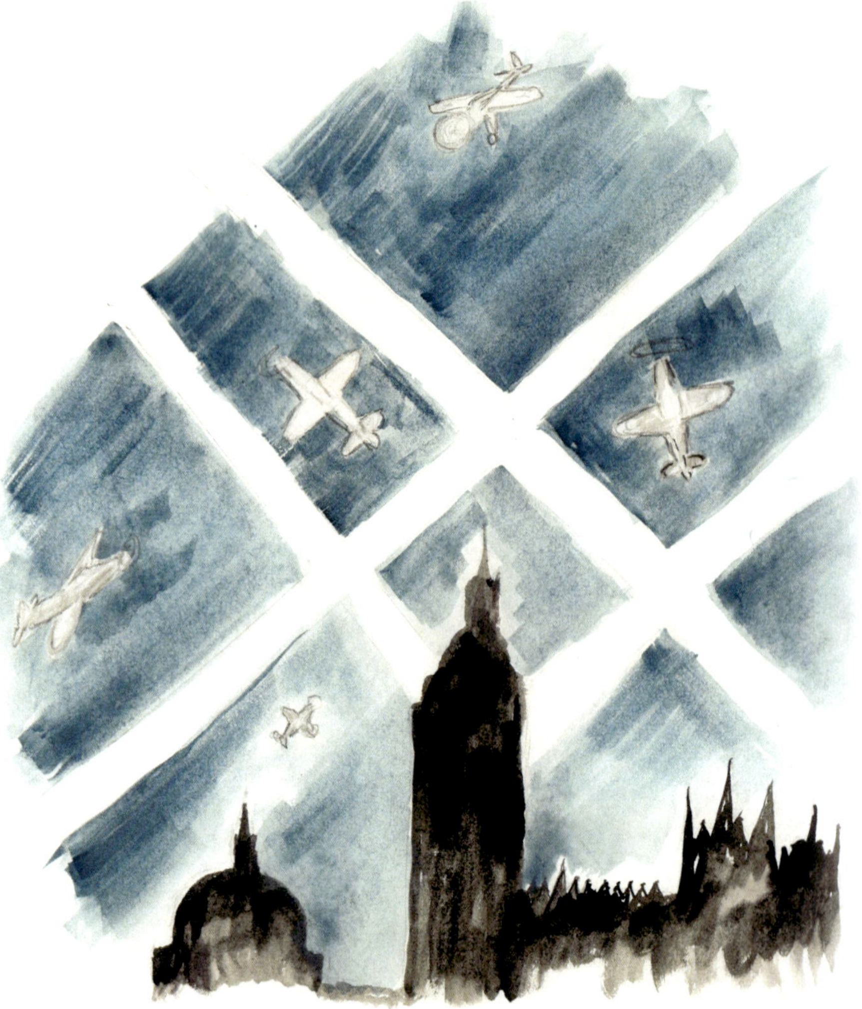

HOME BASE

FLOWER–BOUND

Your mother's daughter certainly you were.
You shared her colour-matching cans and can'ts.
You were obsessed with gardening, just like her.
For special days, friends gave you potted plants.
Ken led the way, but chose exotic blooms.
Few followed him. You hinted at your choices
by placements of the pots in various rooms,
and wished that flowers, like cats, were given voices.

You planted birthday beds of friendship flowers.
You kept the garden well; it kept you well.
You thought and planned it all your waking hours.
Even the gaudy weeds would cast their spell.
You left wild flowers to edge through cracks like hope
and loved the ways that they could interlope.

TAKEN AS READ * (for Viv)

Your first words when two cars struck the bungalow:
"What have they done to my roses?" trembling in shock.
Dusk, neighbours, paramedics, workmen, the law.
The drivers surely drunk, speeding or berserk.

Tearful but talking, you called the Christmas plant
'the paracetamol' – a name that raised a smile.
At dawn next day, you dropped dead. You'd hoped and planned
to end at home while gardening or cooking a meal.

Your green fingers locked away to keep
poinsettia – friends called it paracetamol
in memory of you.
                        They say men, left to cope
with wives away, fail first one, then all
the houseplants. Yet, red-fingered now, I beckon
eyes to your garden with its blazing beacon.

CRYPTOGRAPH

That's where it was, back of the linen drawer,
my favourite snap of us. Clearly not yours.
It must be holidays but where? And why indoors?
Where was it? Who took it? Some friend on the tour.
You'd never hinted what got under your skin.
Was it the tour? Me? Tour friend? The place?
Or was it just this version of your face?
Whichever, you never tossed it in the bin.

Ah well, I'll prop us in the light, my dear,
where it may crack a chink in memory's door.
But fresh eyes find no key-code to unlock
the snap, however hard or where they look.
The camera cannot lie. The lens is silent.
The past develops the opaquest sealant.

MEMENTOS*

One friend considered dream a bonus life.
Two for the price of one? A con, I reckoned,
bogus. Who'd opt for extra storm and strife?
One's the allotted span. Why risk a second?
Yet, love, you wake up in my dreaming head,
and, in that low and lovely voice you'd had,
murmur the words unspoken that we heard
when each lay far too nakedly to hide.

Love, oh, my love, no bonus dream was this.
Your handcrafts, trinkets, treasures absent you from me.
I'm talking to your silence all the time.
Nothing enlivens. They cannot reminisce.
I mooch around among them like a zombie.
– Remember the weird lightning, that Ventnor climb?

TALKING SHOP

A LAY OF THE LAST RETAINER*

On college, clubs, and Anglo-Saxon verse,
on unforeseen long life, a lively career,
old schemes, old scars, I look back and curse.
An Anglo-Saxon 'scop' pricks up my ear:
'that passed...' which leaves me facing down a frail
old age to come, as he concludes his remark:
"this will." Fast forward to system fail.
My comrades all are gone into the velvet dark.

They don't die young. The ancient Greeks weren't right.
Those whom the gods do love are never ill,
die painlessly and quick, their courses run.
Age, age into the nighing of the night.
'Unarm, Eros, the long day's task is... done'
That passed. And so this waste of words soon will.

BAR-ROOM CHAT

'Once written, twice high' you'd tell us in the bar,
'the finalising word transmogrifies
drafts of the poem into draughts of beer.'
'Real poems are rare and seldom earn the fizz.'
'Take care of the sense, who was it said?
And the sounds will look after themselves.'
'If you need a second page, you won't succeed.'
Your namesakes are too orderly on my shelves.

Your books. I wish we'd shared not words, but lives,
though poets live as exiles in their own heads.
A generation is an ebbing tide that leaves
flotsam and jetsam wrack, lapsed likelihoods.
Our printed books are disembodied headstones round
a garden sited on deconsecrated ground.

SOME DREAM TEAM*

What now? Why infiltrate my dreams, old rival?
Time past since either might apologize;
our squandered talents well beyond retrieval.
Well, do you dream me up? No way to liaise.
You'd swear I've conned you to my dreaming shires.
Two sparrow-hawks, vying for scattered peanuts.
Don't try it on still, hamming up fresh airs.
You can't change the past with cheapjack penance.

You dead? Why else me, your dream haunts,
me, who would pooh-pooh how you'd advance
your obfuscations? You never take our hints.
I'm not the only one your verbiage can't convince.
Obscurantist, your printed voice is dumbed.
'Be thou a spirit of grace or goblin damned?'

THE CUTTING EDGE OF DREAM

Some people say they choose their sleeping dreams
but seldom name their favourite nightly stars.
How chosen? Series, episodes, themes?
You'd soon be bored with wish-list bars, spas, cars.
Who'd go for pipe-dreams, castles in Spain?
    – Don't ask if I sleep well. The dreams are hell.
Friends missed, loves lost, years back, show up again,
recapping hopes that daylight will dispel.

Yet I am powerless; the dreams choose me,
and turn to nightmare as the daylight beams.
Frail rages at the vulture face of time
and its circling closer round the chance to be
or not... Late friends, if I could choose my dreams,
we'd all be dreamt together in our prime.

IDLE TALK

The inner ear still hearkens to their voices.
The echoes break the silence of the room,
words of their idiosyncratic choices,
the shards of conversations to resume.
Some names escape me. Eileen would 'vamoose'
when Greg set forth 'on notion-going trips'.
Murphy was keen to redefine 'wayzgoose'.
Steven would threaten 'to launch a thousand quips'.

Presences shadow me around the house.
I stop and launch your idiolects aloud,
my dead fellows in rhyme, for old times' sake.
We swear our coined expletives as we grouse
at the tripewriter, hypewriter, gripewriter crowd
that makes our cursive, penurious fingers ache.

DREAM ON

Some sleep-research concludes we never dream
of our own dead. But that is not the case.
Two decades dead yet still your voice and face
appear in dreams expounding our fond old theme
of poems, not verse, our lifelong two man team,
touchstones and quotes criss-cross our share of space.
Fresh theories of yours my memory could not retrace
to past discussions. New, as it would seem.

After a dream has had your latest say,
a settled calm pervades the living day.
It's strange since dreams must be soliloquy.
Your voice must be some ventriloquial me.
Despite the doubtful memory of dream,
I miss you. Which of us were we in our late, late team?

AFTERWORD*

I stand once more, still puzzling in my hall.
It's all your doing, my lifelong, childhood friend;
your 'Jiver' gouache on the right-hand wall;
opposite, done three years before your end,
my portrait, mouth penned in a rollneck top.
This nubile 'Jiver', pictured in your teens.
I wonder now what words you feigned to stop,
stuck here between your youth and age. Two has-beens.

You'd had me write the intros to one-man shows;
So, is this rollneck joke some mute dissent?
Or was my verse the butt of your intent?
– But then your choice of books was always prose.
Should the eye catch in 'Jiver' a voyeur Chad?
– I've punned on 'penned'. We're quits. Each has been had.

DRAGONIAN MEASURES

THE FIRST WELSH DRAGON

Once upon a time
> There was a Welsh Dragon.

He was the colour of lime
> And lived in a green wagon.

He did not like his colour,
> This young unusual Dragon.

He thought the green much duller
> And nothing much to brag on.

He wanted to be red
> And really Welsh Dragony.

This problem vexed his head
> And gave him quite an agony.

He'd like to look like carrot
> Or any shade of scarlet,

Crimson, magenta, claret,
> Vermilion or garnet.

But how do you turn red

        Except with some embarrassment?

This problem vexed his head.

        He suffered aweful harassment.

He hated most the billows

        From tongues of flame he spouted

Since all were green as willows

        And lettuce newly sprouted.

He dreamed a pillar-box

        Might be the thing to wear

With national rugby socks

        And through the slot he'd flare.

He thought a tin of paint

        Might simply do the trick

If used with some restraint.

        And mixed with powdered brick.

He chose a rose-red flush

    By checking through the lipstick.

He used a four-inch brush

    And stirred it with a dipstick.

Alas, he could not reach

    The bit between his shoulders

(Which stayed a shade of peach).

    His breath went out in smoulders.

In dismal deep despair

    He flew off to Llanberis

To find a herbalist there

    And he suggested cranberries.

He said a pint a day

    And several baths per fortnight

Would be the painless way

    To make him look and snort right.

But first the paint must vanish.

  And that might be a pain.

He'd have to be quite mannish

  To scrub himself quite plain.

The Dragon braced himself

  For it to hurt a fair bit.

He scraped himself with Delft

  But, best of all, Welsh rarebit.

Well, like a desperado,

  He hid till he had done it

And seemed an avocado

  Or gooseberries in a punnet.

And next he started drinking

  The pints of cranberry juice.

Bathing in it and sinking

  And then he turned dull puce.

He thought that he was winning
> And so he bathed each day

(He'd scarcely need clean linen.)
> And golloped pints away.

Oh, red, red, red, was the dragon
> And filled with pink delight.

He never forgot his flagon
> Of cranberry each night.

Vermilion, crimson, russet,
> Burgundy, cinnabar,

The cranberry nicely does it,
> The Dragon is a Star.

And when you see the flag on
> Any building now

You'll see the famous dragon
> As red as he knows how.

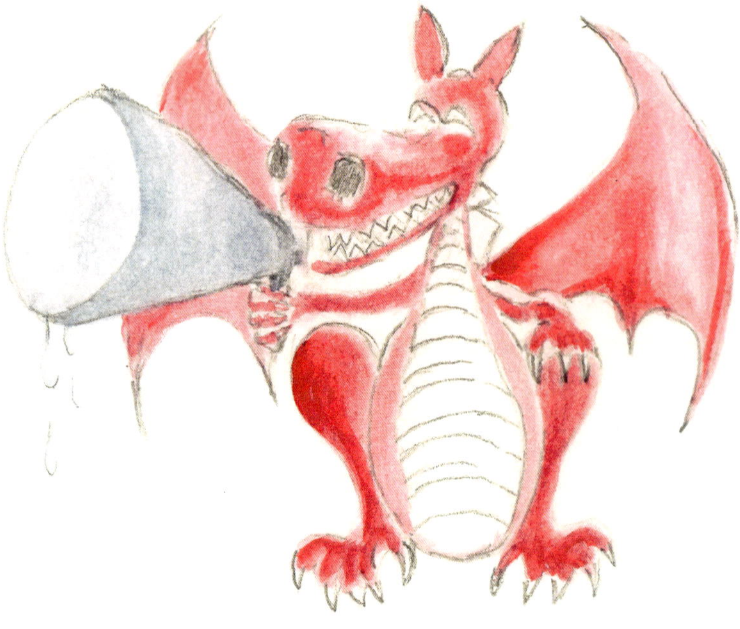

SMOKY

A youngish dragon nicknamed Smoky
      Was very keen, red hot on rugby.
He cheered his team till he was croaky
      And yelling louder was too struggly.

Some fans were worried by young Smoky
      And very fearful for their rugby
Since Smoky's cheers were most heat-stroky,
      Stinging to eyes as would a bug be.

But others thought him okey-dokey
      And jolly useful at the rugby.
They thought it splendidly good-bloky
      To warm the terraces so snugly.

So all went well for young red Smoky
      And he was welcome at the rugby.
But then the weather turned quite soaky
      And gathering rain clouds looked quite ugly.

The roof was closed and poor young Smoky

        Must hardly breathe a flame at rugby.

His cheering would have made it choky,

        Might burn the roof and he'd a mug be.

So fans whipped round and bought young Smoky

        An ice-cooled megaphone for rugby,

Told him: you cheer but keep it low-key,

        So risks of fire would be less troubly.

Yet still fans worried over Smoky

        And had to calm themselves for rugby.

To stop themselves from getting choky

        They brought in beer, got bubbly-clubby.

But that was not much good for Smoky.

        This liquid cheering at the rugby

Would turn his tail too joky-poky

        And damp his cheers and turn things fuggy.

But that's a thing some blamed on Smoky,

    The need for drinking at the rugby

And why the fans came home so brokely

    As would a cracked and empty jug be.

But fans need cooling down from Smoky

    Who gets hot-headed at the rugby.

For their excuse he's okey-dokey

    And so they booze away quite smugly.

And then the match is won and Smoky,

    Fans and followers of rugby

Celebrate with the karaoke

    And things become quite glug-glug-glugly.

Pub-singing, though, they banned since Smoky

    Might burn or wreck their favourite pub, see.

No songs from Smokey, no hokey-cokey.

    But he's still mascot at the rugby.

(And now to end this tale of Smoky,

    The famous mascot at the rugby,

I'll tell you all these rhymes are trochee –

    Which means they rhyme on vowels doubly

    And rhymers find that tricky-troubly.)

DRAGON FLIES?

Why do dragons need their wings?
    I've never seen one flying.
No need like birds, if a cat springs,
    to tease it by sky-highing.

Maybe they use them more as fans
    to flap their fires forwards
but jets of fire and vast wingspans
    would thrust them back and floorwards

The sun's their rival fiery beast,
    they think. They see it creep
out of the darkness in the east
    and know it's time to sleep.

They much prefer the stone-cold moon
    and so they're fly-by-night.
And darkness cannot come too soon
    for them to take to flight.

They looked for lakes with floating moons.
    Their breath blindfolds their eyes.
They'd need to man hot-air balloons.
    Since then no dragon flies.

ON THE MARGINS
<   >

GREETINGS
When old, you don't want greeting cards too treacly
and need a get-well-soon card almost weekly.
You hardly bother celebrating birthdays
that egg you on to the encroaching earth days.

INSPIRATION
Poets are born and not made liars.
Poetry is the fiend that lies like truth.
It's had me in its thraldom since my youth.
When all you see, hear, smell, taste and touch inspires.

VIRILE VIRUSES
Microbes are lords of us.
Medics have wards of us.
And Earth has hordes of us.
Time makes frauds of us.

DRESS–SENSE
The dress of western men fills me with loathing.
It's most uncomfortable as a form of clothing.
Waist belts are absolutely useless trouser holders.
It's clear that clothes should hang from upright shoulders.
But you won't get most men wearing frocks.
But what is wrong with medieval smocks,
especially if matched with Scottish socks?

PROSPECTS
Young we were wild, mating, nut-brown.
It's second childhood now, waiting for shut-down.

COMMUNICATION
The body's handed in its notice
The aches and pains acutely quote this.

SOLILOQUY
The fool hath said in his heart there is no god.
But that soliloquy is not so odd.
For, if he spoke too often or too loud,
he would be pestered by the godly crowd.

GEOSOPHY

The Gods are not a fact.
Hard facts have far more tact.
They wait until they're seen
to tell us what they mean.

WINTER SOLSTICE

Traditions call it midwinter day
and though the ancients planted henges astronomically
the solstitial name's an anomaly.
Not midwinter. It *starts* the winter fray.

TRANSLATION WORKSHOP

Civis Romanus sum.
Of Rome am I a citizen.
Of Rome a citizen I am.
Of Rome I am a citizen.
I am of Rome a citizen.
A citizen am I of Rome.
A citizen I am of Rome.
A citizen of Rome am I.
A Roman citizen am I.
A Roman citizen I am.
I am a Roman citizen.
A Roman citizen, me.
A citizen of Rome, me.
Me, a Roman citizen.
Roman citizen, me.
Citizen of Rome, me.
I'm a citizen of Rome.
I'm a Roman citizen.
Me, a Roman.
Roman, me.
My name is Palmerston,
Civis Britannicus sum.

ENVOI

No: just lounging in your kaftan,
   your lithe fingers softly holding
smoothing, stroking the long-furred kitten,
   you wouldn't have to die to haunt me.

Your low, low voice that used to call me,
   so low when someone else might panic,
that alto voice that never calmed me
   till I find you, gardening, still, then pointing.

You haunt my inner ear and hindsight.
   Your low, low call in pre-dawn darkness,
and me, too frail and useless, single-handed.
   Silent goodbyes, my life-long darling.

NOTES

Blackout

As the bomber flies, our wartime house was about three miles from Vickers aircraft factory where my father worked. It was also two miles from the main London-Portsmouth Southsea railway line, and about the same from the Thames. These were often targets or guides for German planes.

Richard II, Forty

This is a translation of a poem by Louis Aragon, written in 1940 after the Fall of France. The poet is referring to Shakespeare's 'Richard II' play where Richard was forced to abdicate in favour of Henry Bolingbroke. It's likely that the Nazis did not catch these references, though the reference to Coventry may have been a reference to the German bombing of the city. Aragon does not use any punctuation in the poem.

Whereabouts

Our house was opposite Smith's fields and farm. The doodlebugs were supposed to be safe so long as you could hear their motors. Silence meant they were going to blow up.

Taken as Read

The poinsettia was a gift from our neighbour a few months before my wife died.

Mementos

We were riding a tandem up the steep hill just north of Ventnor, neither of us had seen lightning at sea before.

A Lay of the Last Retainer

Last Retainer: In Anglo-Saxon culture, to survive your lord and comrades in battle was regarded as dishonourable. And no other lord would have been likely to accept you.

L.4 A 'scop', this is an Anglo-Saxon word for a poet.

L.8 This line is a quotation from Tennyson

L.12 This is a parody of Dylan Thomas's line - from his 'Do Not Go Gentle' villanelle 'Rage, rage against the dying of the light.'

L.13 This is a line in *Antony & Cleopatra*, Act 4.14 L.35 This line was spoken just before Antony's suicide. Eros, the name of Antony's servant, is also the name of the Greek god of sexual love – this may be Shakespeare referring to the ending of Antony's affair with Cleopatra.

Some Dream Team
L.14 This is L.140 in Act 1.4 from *Hamlet*. It is Hamlet's opening remark to the ghost of his father, reflecting his own doubts. It is his query between the Catholic view that ghosts are unquiet souls seeking some release from the living. The Protestant view was that ghosts were devils in disguise trying to entrap souls of the living.

Afterword
Chad or Mr. Chad was a wartime graffiti item, a bald head with big eyes and a long nose hanging over a fence with the comments underneath "what, no...", a comment on wartime and postwar shortages.

Translation Workshop
In 1850, Lord Palmerston was in trouble with his colleagues and the House of Lords for his handling of the Don Pacifico incident and used this Latin sentence made famous by St. Paul's use of it. He changed it of course; to Civis Britannicus sum.

ABOUT THE AUTHOR

Peter Dale has been writing and translating poetry for more than fifty years. Some of his poems may be read and heard on the National Poetry Archive (available online: www.poetryarchive.org) CD: ISBN 1 905556 12 8. His collected poems may be read in *Diffractions: New and Collected Poems* published in 2012 by Anvil Press Poetry (now managed by Carcanet Press, more information available online: www.carcanet.co.uk/cgi-bin/indexer?owner_id=1462). He has published a limited edition book, *Aquatints,* with Minilith Press in 2014. His most recent books of poems are *Local Habitation*, and *Diffractions: New and Collected Poems*. He has also jointly written a book on dowsing with John Bowers, *Grounded*, Minilith Press, 2014, who also publish his current books of verse, *Aquatints* and *Penumbral*.

His verse translation of Tristan Corbière *Wry-Blue Loves* received a Poetry Book Society recommendation in 2005. Of his book, *Da Capo,* Philip Hoy wrote 'Dale deserves to be ranked as one of the great poets of relationships, a worthy heir to Tennyson, Meredith, Patmore, Browning, Clough, Hardy, Graves, Frost.'

'His poems are mostly short (he doesn't waste words), and inviting, accessible; and yet they carry a depth of thought and reference that means that they can tease and catch in the mind long after the first reading. His is a very individual voice, and a strikingly consistent voice; but it deals with such a range of reflective material that it always subtly surprises' – R.V. Bailey